THE NEW LIFE LIBRARY

ALEXANDER TECHNIQUE

THE NEW LIFE LIBRARY

ALEXANDER TECHNIQUE

REGAIN YOUR NATURAL POISE AND ALLEVIATE STRESS

MICHÈLE MAC DONNELL

SELECT EDITIONS

Select Editions imprint specially produced for Selectabook Limited

Produced by Anness Publishing Limited
Hermes House
88–89 Blackfriars Road
London SE1 8HA

A CIP catalogue record for this book is available from the British Library.

Publisher: Joanna Lorenz
Managing Editor: Helen Sudell
Designer: Lilian Lindblom, Photographer: Dave Jordan
Editorial Reader: Marion Wilson, Illustrator: Anna Koska
Models: Simon Berkowitz, Gloria Else, Dee Townsend

1 3 5 7 9 10 8 6 4 2

Publisher's Note
The reader should not regard the recommendations, ideas and techniques expressed and described in this book as substitutes for the advice of a qualified medical practitioner or other qualified professional. Any use to which the recommendations, ideas and techniques are put is at the reader's sole discretion and risk.

Contents

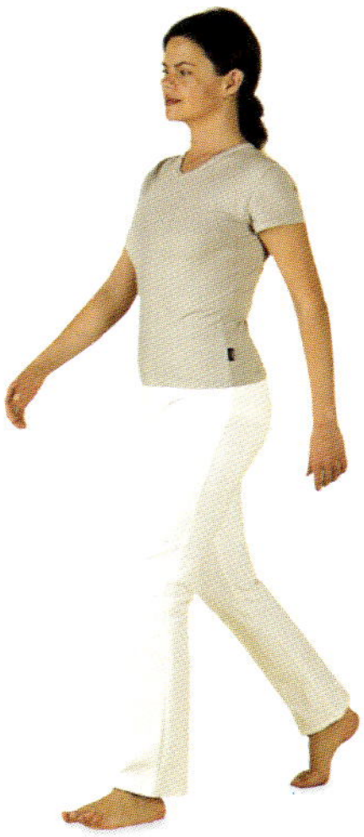

Introduction

People tend to associate the Alexander Technique with relaxation, alternative medicine, body massage and, in particular, with "posture". They are often unable to be more precise than that.

One way towards a clearer understanding of the Technique is to begin by stating what it is not. The Alexander Technique does not train its teachers to make a medical diagnosis of their students. Neither does it focus on or encourage any division between the mind and the body. There is a popular image of intellectuals as dishevelled professors with rounded shoulders and a collapsed body frame. People with healthy bodies are often linked with sports such as body-building or perhaps with dance. The Alexander Technique, however, believes in the indivisibility of the mind and the body, in their psycho-physical unity. It employs the terms "use" and "misuse" to describe the various ways in which the mind and the body work together to perform everyday activities.

Above all, though, the Technique's main objective is to encourage people to use themselves, their bodies and minds, more effectively in their day-to-day lives.

How Can the Technique be Useful?

An understanding of the psycho-physical system as a whole is essentially focused on the co-ordination of the head, the neck and the back. If we interfere with the sophisticated and subtle relationship between these three regions, it can become distorted and strained. When this happens, the system as a whole becomes affected and "misuse" follows. The Technique's preventive role is an efficient tool to maintain tone and general well-being, once it is integrated in our systems.

◀ Observe how this model is using herself to bend. She is respecting the relationship between her head, her neck and her back.

▶ Here the model is standing. She is poised. Her weight is evenly distributed.

The Teacher-Pupil Relationship

Teachers of the Alexander Technique seek to establish a relationship based on trust. They use their hands to encourage better co-ordination in their pupils, while at the same time giving verbal instruction and explanation. They note if their pupils are "shortening" (stooping) or "lengthening" (maintaining their full stature), if they are tensing or releasing, and how they respond to different stimuli. In time, pupils develop a better awareness of their habitual patterns of misuse. They gradually learn to change their habits, and ultimately have a conscious choice of how to respond in an appropriate manner, both physically and mentally.

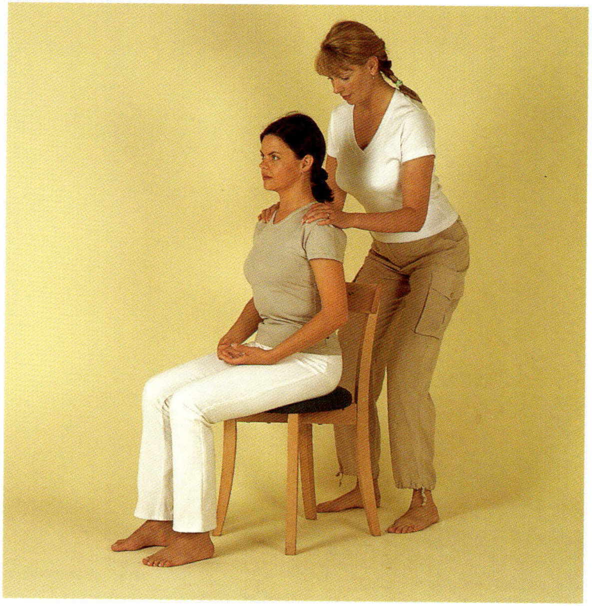

▲ Observe how the pupil is encouraged to lengthen and widen with the teacher's hands.

Who Can Benefit from the Technique?

The people who benefit from the Technique come from all walks of life. They may be motivated by specific symptoms resulting from "misuse", which can be endemic, and are therefore seeking relief from aches and pains, headaches, backaches, stiff necks and frozen shoulders. They may be musicians, athletes, teachers, dentists, young mothers; anyone, in fact, who overstrains one area of their body on a regular basis through their work or private life. Alternatively, prospective pupils may simply experience a general lack of poise and energy, which affects them both physically and mentally. They may wish to improve their overall co-ordination and body posture.

Although the Technique's main objective is prevention rather than cure, it does help to improve posture and relieve related pain. It can assist people with stress-related illnesses such as respiratory and gastro-intestinal problems, as well as psychosomatic conditions. It can help those who suffer from psychological distress, such as depression, as well as facilitating recovery from accidents and injuries. It can assist people with mechanical problems, such as frozen shoulder, tennis elbow and arthritis. It helps promote muscle tone and general well-being as well as encouraging poise and flexibility.

To conclude, this book does not set out to be used as a substitute for practical sessions with a qualified Alexander Technique teacher. However, the following pages may enable more people to gain a better understanding of the Technique and its benefits. If in any doubt about your physical health, consult a medical practitioner before embarking on any of the procedures in this book.

How Lessons Can Help

- Encourage the release and prevention of unnecessary wear on, and muscular tension in, the body.
- Aid breathing.
- Improve posture and ease of movement.
- Make people more aware of their patterns of misuse, their habits and how they can consciously change them.
- Enable people to preserve their energy with a minimum of effort.
- Bring about improved physical and mental health.

Francis Matthias Alexander (1869-1955)

Francis Matthias Alexander was born in Tasmania in 1869. In 1896 he moved to Sydney and became a professional reciter of dramatic pieces. (In the days before radio and television it was common for an actor to recite extracts from a book from the stage to a theatre audience.) Performing alone for two hours or more in this manner was often quite a strain. He regularly found that he was losing his voice towards the end of a performance, despite following his doctor's advice.

After a long process of self-examination, and with the help of mirrors, he discovered a technique that cured his voice without any medical aid. This became known as the Alexander Technique.

▲ Francis Matthias Alexander.

In 1904, Alexander moved to London where he introduced the Alexander Technique. A class was established there in 1924 for teaching children, and September 1930 saw the establishment of the first training course for teachers of the Technique. This tradition has continued to this day, and all teachers of the Technique are required to undertake a three-year full-time training course to diploma (professional certificate) standard.

By 1937 the Technique had become well-known, and 19 doctors, all of whom had practical experience of the work, collectively petitioned the British Medical Association for the inclusion of the Alexander Technique in the medical curriculum. A copy of this application appeared in the form of a letter in the British Medical Journal on 27 May 1937.

During the Second World War Alexander moved to the United States, then came back to England where he continued to teach until his death in 1955. He wrote four books on the subject: *Man's Supreme Inheritance* (1910), *Constructive Control of the Individual* (1923), *The Use of the Self* (1932) and *The Universal Constant in Living* (1941).

In 1958 the Society of Teachers of the Alexander Technique – STAT – was established, which today has over 1,200 members worldwide.

The Alexander Technique and its Principles

The Head, Neck, Back Relationship or Primary Control

"Misuse" occurs by contracting the muscles of the neck and pulling the head back and down into the shoulders. This has the effect of compressing the spine and narrowing and shortening the stature, and causes unnecessary tensions throughout the body.

Alexander discovered that the relationship between the head, the neck and the back (or "primary control"), mechanically controlled movement and co-ordination throughout the whole body. To make ourselves aware of this consciously in our daily activities is the basis of good use.

"Use affects functioning."
F. M. Alexander

▶ Observe how this little boy is standing and looking up slightly. He is naturally well co-ordinated and his head is balanced on top of his spine.

End-gaining

The concept of end-gaining is extremely important in the work of Alexander Technique teachers.

Alexander realized that the habits he was encountering were far more deep-rooted and powerful than he had at first thought. The most serious of these was the tendency to try to react impulsively – end-gaining. End-gaining means reacting immediately and too quickly to a stimulus, without thinking. You respond by wanting something to happen, and become interested in the end result instead of being in the present. A typical example is if you are going to be late for an appointment and start to worry about the consequences. You get worked up during this process, forgetting that you might be sitting on a train, and that things are happening around you. In effect you are letting your thoughts take the situation into the future, instead of being in the "here and now", in the present.

"Possession of property…a means to happiness not as an end."
Thomas Jefferson

Consequences of End-gaining

Cutting yourself off from your environment has inevitable consequences for body positioning. It tends to lead to a pulling back of the head, a rounding of the back, a tightening of the legs and a loss of connection between the arms and the back. The gaze becomes fixed, the breath held. Essentially, the whole person is affected, both in mind and in body.

Means-whereby

Alexander suggests an alternative: using one's "means-whereby". To put Alexander's conclusion into context, in the example opposite, if we accept that we cannot change circumstances, that they are inevitable, we can change our approach to our bodies and allow ourselves to experience something new. It is then possible to learn to be in the moment rather than the past or the future, and to maintain a sense of inner balance and unity.

▶ Observe how this woman is slumped as she walks with her dog, depicting poor posture.

Faculty Sensory Appreciation or Awareness

Alexander's next important realization was that habits were not just habits of action, but that there existed habits of feeling which underlay habitual actions. What he felt was different from what was happening. It is not uncommon for new pupils to think that they are walking upright, when actually they are hunched. When a teacher releases their bodies, they might feel twisted or think they are leaning backwards or forwards, when in fact they are straight and vertical for the first time since infancy.

▲ Animals are spontaneous in their actions. As this dog runs, his head and spine are perfectly aligned enabling his legs to move freely under him.

Inhibition

In its physiological sense, inhibition means a healthy and natural control of inappropriate reactions, without any sense of suppressing spontaneity.

Alexander discovered that if he managed to stop himself from behaving in his habitual way, he could choose how he wished to respond to a stimulus. If someone rings the doorbell, your immediate response may be to go straight to the door. In doing so, you will be responding habitually, automatically and subconsciously. If you stop yourself responding automatically, you can choose consciously how you will approach the door with the minimum of effort.

Direction or Thinking in Activity

Directions are signals or orders given by the brain to parts of the body, prior to, or during, specific physical action. It is possible to alter these signals in order to promote positive change. Specific directions are discussed in the practical sections, where they are referred to either as "primary directions", involving the head, neck and back relationship, or as "secondary directions", relating to actions or movements performed by other parts of the body. The combination of direction and inhibition enables one to transform habitual ways of moving and gradually eliminate old patterns of misuse.

Primary Directions

Think of allowing the neck to be free.
To allow the head to go forward and up.
To allow the back to lengthen and widen.

▶ Note how this model is walking. Her head, her neck and her back are aligned. Her arms are free to move.

Our Natural Poise

Young children are usually alert and balanced, which enables them to move gracefully and effortlessly, without strain. They have not yet lost their natural poise and co-ordination. Look at the following pictures:

▼ As this child crawls, her head, her neck and her back are perfectly aligned, and lead her whole body into movement. Her eyes are alert and focused on something out of her reach. Her intent is to go towards it.

▲ As this child carries his cuddly toy close to his body his whole body lengthens.

◀ Observe how this child is sitting on the floor. She has maintained her alignment as she uses her eyes to look down towards the floor, without tilting her head down.

▶ Note how this child is using his joints to squat and how he holds the plastic bag effortlessly.

Later, in adult life, we rarely see the poise and freedom of movement that are so characteristic of young children.

◀ See how this model is misusing himself. He is leaning over to the right, shortening and creating an imbalance in his body.

▲ Note how the model is slumping on the bench and how his legs are stretched out, offering him little support.

Putting the Alexander Technique into Practice

A certain degree of commitment is paramount during a course of lessons. It takes time to change, to release unnecessary muscular tension and to re-educate the system. Some pitfalls are inevitable. One may try to do the directions instead of thinking them, or wish to give up because one cannot see anything significant occurring.

Another tendency is to try to get into a position without bothering to go through the thinking process. This results in a stereotyped posture achieved through imitation, rather than through an application of the directions to the desired movement. The following sections attempt to identify the main procedures that we use most often in daily life. (The use of the word "procedure" is deliberate, as it avoids the suggestion of a mind-body split and maintains a sense of psycho-physical unity.) The emphasis throughout is on the means of achieving these procedures with the minimum of muscular tension and effort.

A course of lessons could be compared to learning a new skill or language. Dedication and determination are a sure basis for success!

The following chapters will illustrate how one can put into practice these procedures in everyday situations.

▲ Note how this model is sitting. She is poised and relaxed, with both feet on the floor.

> "You translate everything, whether physical, mental or spiritual, into muscular tension."
> F. M. Alexander

The Human Skeleton

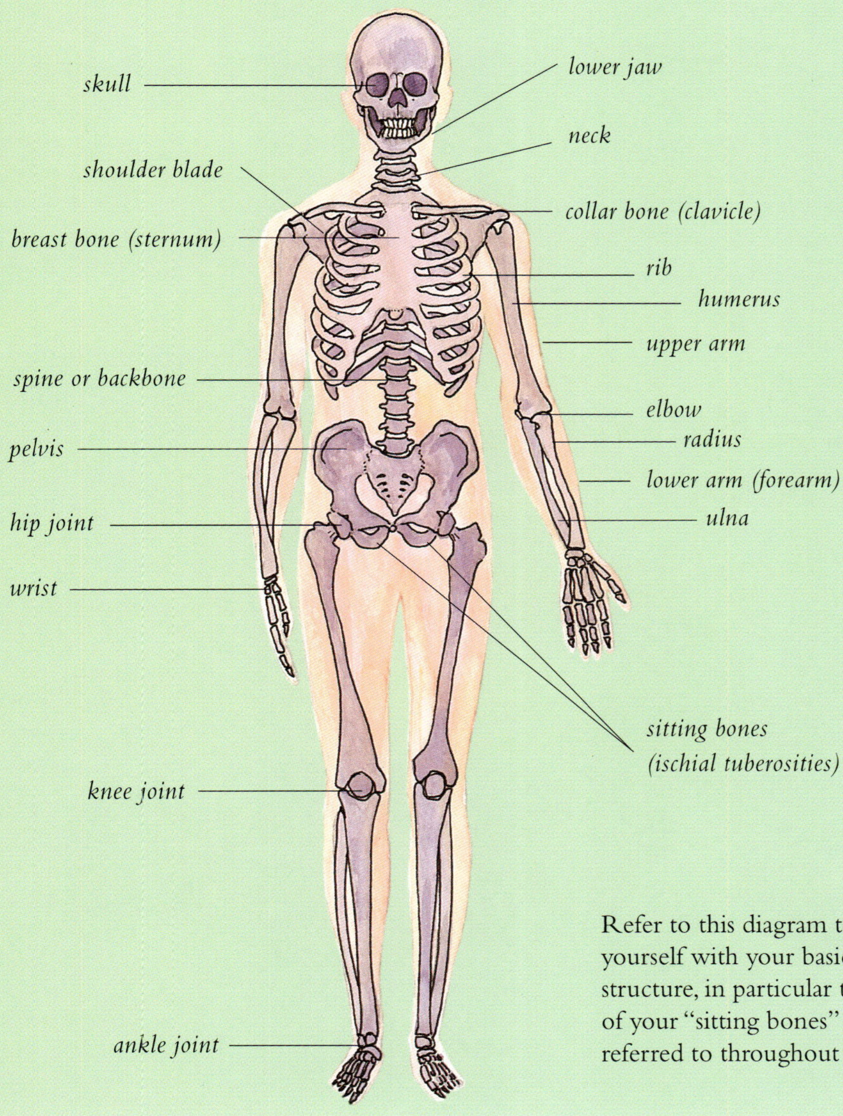

Refer to this diagram to familiarize yourself with your basic bone structure, in particular the location of your "sitting bones" which are referred to throughout this book.

The Semi-supine Position

Standing for long periods compresses the spine. Lying down in a semi-supine position is a way of alleviating unnecessary tensions in the muscles and joints and should be practised every day for at least 20 minutes. It encourages a better awareness of the head, neck, back relationship. This position does not necessarily need monitoring by a teacher and also gives you time for yourself. When in the semi-supine position, the arms are bent and the hands are placed on either side of the torso just below the level of the rib cage to maximise opening and release across the upper arms. The finger-tips are not touching each other.

In this position the head is supported by a certain number of books. The muscles in the back of the neck are thereby encouraged to release, in turn encouraging the muscles to release along the whole length of the spine, allowing the whole torso to lengthen and widen and reducing excessive curvature of the back. The knees are bent and directed towards the ceiling, enabling the muscles in the lower back and the pelvis to release.

> "The question is not of correct position, but of correct co-ordination."
> F. M. Alexander

Try to keep your eyes open. It is preferable to avoid closing them as you will probably find it difficult not to fall asleep, which is not the point of the exercise!

During your daily 20-minute session give yourself the time to practise some directed thoughts to avoid your mind wandering to other important issues. This session can also encourage you to put into practice your skills of observation. A good practice is to go over your primary directions, to notice if you are aware of any tension in your body and to address it without trying to correct it.

▲ If you have too many books your chin will drop towards your chest and you will feel pressure on your throat.

▲ Correspondingly, if you do not have enough books your head will tilt back and will not be properly supported.

MOVING INTO SEMI-SUPINE

To move into the semi-supine position, wear loose clothes for comfort. Avoid tight jeans or trousers, and shoes. It is preferable to lie down on a hard carpeted surface or alternatively on a rug on the floor. Avoid beds or soft surfaces as they will not offer you adequate support. The number of books you need will depend on their thickness and will also vary from person to person.

To lie down on the floor, place the books far enough behind you to give you enough space for the whole of your torso and your bottom. When sitting you can place your hands palms down on the floor behind you to help you lower your back. Take care not to stiffen the arms or hold your breath in the process.

To get up it is preferable to roll over to one side, leading with your eyes rather than your head, and following with your torso and legs. Then place the free hand flat on the floor and go onto all fours. Be careful to maintain the alignment between your head, your neck and your back and not to hold your breath. Walk your hands back so that you move your bottom back towards your heels. Come into a kneeling position before standing.

▲ Make sure that your legs are about hip-width apart and that your knees are directed towards the ceiling. If your knees are falling in, you will probably narrow your lower back and lose the contact between the outer side of your foot and the floor.

▲ If your knees are falling out, you will probably lose the contact between the inner side of your foot and the floor. Check that your legs are balanced. If your heels are too far away from your sitting bones, you will probably start holding in the legs.

KNEELING

Kneeling is useful when you want to get up from the floor after you have been lying down in the semi-supine position. It is also a useful alternative if you find it tiring or difficult to squat for any length of time.

Before you begin to kneel from standing, remember to review your primary directions. Bring your weight back from the middle of your feet on to your heels. Think about releasing in your hips, knees and ankle joints. Leading with your head, allow your torso to bend slightly forwards from your hips as you place one foot behind the other. Go down on to one knee. Then send your torso backwards from your hips to enable you to go on to the other knee.

To go back into standing reverse the procedure by thinking about your primary directions before going into motion.

Avoid placing your hands on your knee as you go from kneeling to standing as you will cause downward pressure on the leg and risk losing the direction of the head leading the body forwards and up.

▲ An example of low kneeling with bottom on heels (correct procedure).

▲ An example of high kneeling with one knee up (correct procedure).

▲ An example of high kneeling with hands pressing down on one knee (incorrect procedure).

USE OF THE EYES

"It's no good shutting your eyes if you're crossing a busy road."
F. M. Alexander

If you observe people when they are standing or walking they often seem to be in a world of their own, unaware of their surrounding environment. When the gaze is fixed, the breathing becomes restricted and there is less freedom in the body. The gaze should be directed towards the outside world, taking in information from outside, so that you are not just concentrating on what is happening within.

One of the strongest habits that a teacher perceives is the tendency of pupils to look down, not with their eyes, but by collapsing from their necks. This is the result of a fundamental misunderstanding of the alignment of the head, the neck and the back and the position of the joints in the body.

Note how the models in the following photographs are using their eyes.

▲ Here the children are using their eyes to look at their toys. They have not disturbed the alignment between their heads, their necks and their backs, thus maintaining their good use.

▲ See how this child is using his eyes to look upwards. He has allowed his head to tilt slightly back without disturbing the fundamental relationship between his head, his neck and his back.

▲ In this position, the model is breaking the alignment between her head, her neck and her back as she looks down, thus using her neck inappropriately.

▲ Note how the model is correctly aligned. She is maintaining her length and her width. Her eyes are alert and taking in her surroundings.

▲ Here the model is breaking at the neckline and pulling her head back to look up, disturbing the alignment between her head, her neck and her back.

SITTING

Most people develop a slouched posture while sitting. They seek support for their backs by leaning against the backs of poorly designed chairs. In so doing they will probably lose the contact between their feet and the floor and encourage an over-exaggerated curve in their lower backs.

When sitting, be aware of the alignment between your head, your neck and your back and check that you are sitting on your sitting bones. Think about widening across your upper arms and lengthening the front of your torso as well as widening across your back. Your legs should be placed hip-width apart, and your knees directed forwards and away from each other over your feet, which are on the floor. Be wary of sitting in one position for long periods as this can cause stiffness and muscular strain.

Observe how you normally sit in a chair and compare the correct procedures shown on the left with those incorrect procedures on the right.

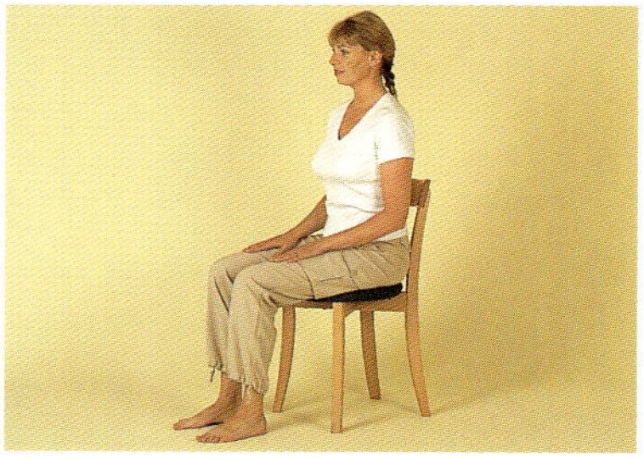

▲ Correct: think of the shoulders going away from each other.

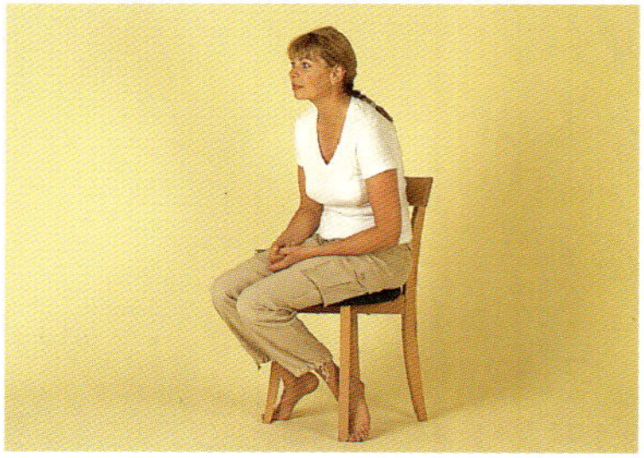

▲ Incorrect: rounded shoulders and feet wrapped around chair legs.

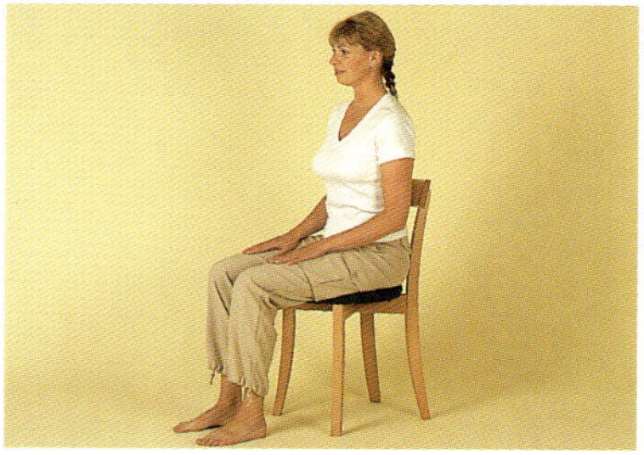

▲ Correct: think of not arching the back and lengthening it.

▲ Incorrect: arching back, folding legs and leaning to one side.

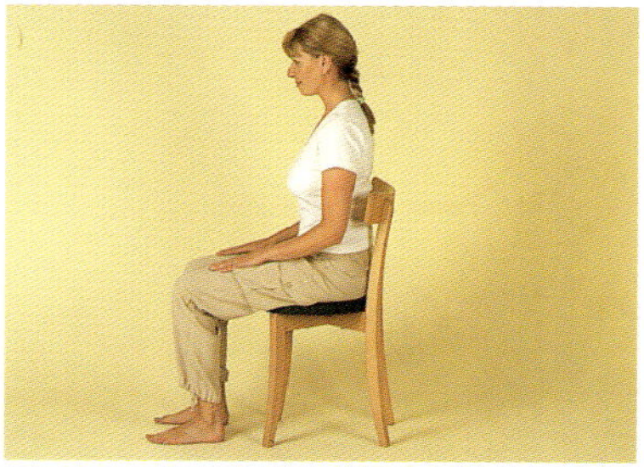

▲ Correct: shoulders dropping.

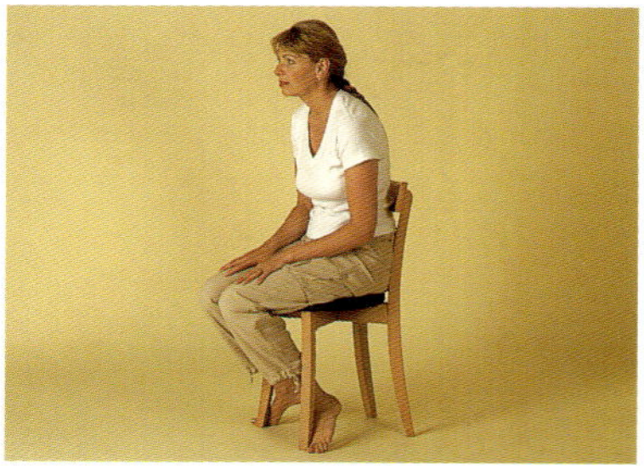

▲ Incorrect: hunched shoulders.

From Sitting to Standing

To stand, your legs should be placed hip-width apart. Avoid pushing up with your legs. Make sure that your feet are flat and not placed so far forwards that coming up to standing is difficult. Remember to lead with the head.

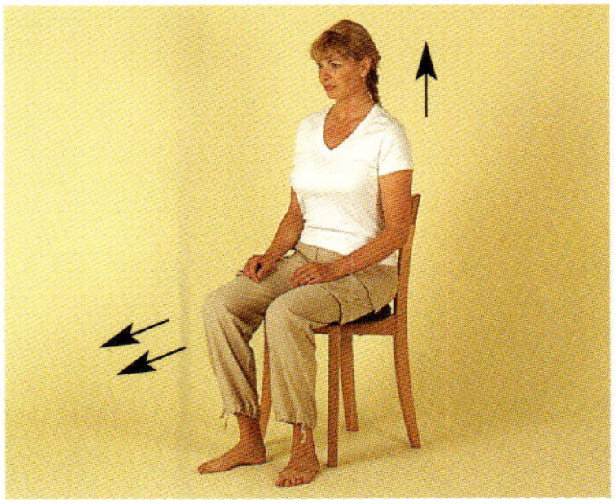

▲ Here the model is poised.

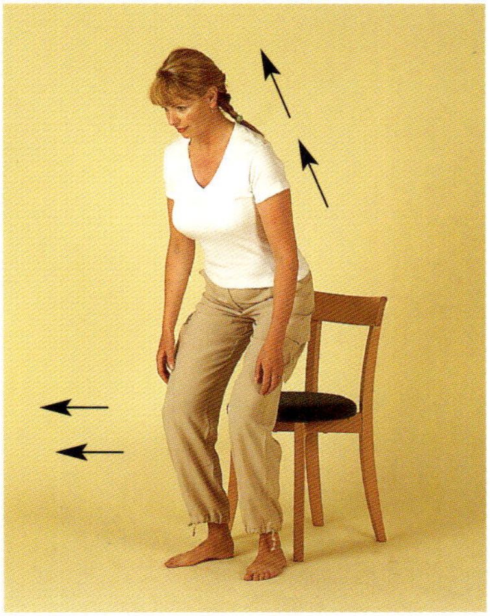

▲ As she stands she has not lost the alignment between her head, neck and back. She is maintaining length and width across her upper arms, hingeing from the hip joints and sending her knees forwards and away over her feet. This encourages length and width throughout the body.

▲ Avoid pushing up with your hands on your thighs as you stand. You are likely to create unnecessary downward pressure on your legs.

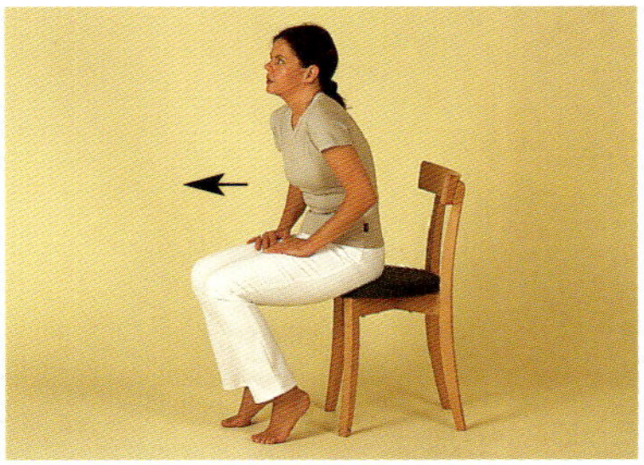

▲ Avoid pushing up with your legs as you stand. You are likely to pull the head back and down on the spine.

▲ If you hunch your shoulders, round your back and hold in your arms, you will have to use far more energy to stand up.

STANDING

People adopt a wide range of postures when standing. At one extreme is the "sergeant-major" stance, which people mistake for "correct" posture. In fact, pulling the shoulders back leads to narrowing across the back, holding in the chest restricts the breathing, and bracing the knees and holding in the feet creates unnecessary muscular tension throughout the system. At the other end of the spectrum is the position often favoured and adopted by many of us, whereby the body's weight is placed on one leg or the other. This creates an imbalance throughout the body, as the right- or left-hand side of the torso inevitably shortens. While standing, it is important to keep your balance on both feet. Check that your weight is resting on the middle of your feet.

A good way of maintaining this is to be aware of the ball under your big toe, your little toe and your heel. Review your primary directions, paying particular attention to your length and width. Keep your eyes alert and do not hold your breath.

▲ While standing, avoid leaning your arm on your hip, as your weight will become unevenly distributed and you will shorten on one side of your torso.

▲ Note how the model is poised. She is aligned. Her eyes are not fixed, but alert.

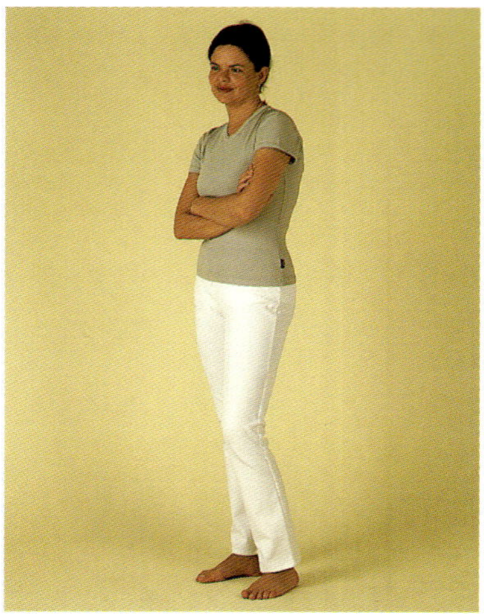

▲ Avoid folding your arms as you stand as their weight is likely to drag round your shoulders and your arms will lose their connection with your back.

FROM STANDING TO SITTING

▲ Look at how the model is standing, poised and alert.

▲ Note how she hinges from the hip joints, maintaining the alignment between her head, her neck and her back.

▲ While sitting on the chair, she is balanced on both sitting bones and continuing to maintain her alignment.

When sitting down from a standing position it is important to think of releasing the knees so as to avoid slumping in the chair, and to maintain your alignment so as not to disturb the relationship between your head, your neck and your back. Otherwise you will affect the alignment of the body and create unnecessary tension in your muscles as you move. Equally, you will risk losing your sense of balance and direction.

▲ Note how the model's head is pulled back. She has lost her alignment. She is creating downward pressure on her spine.

▲ It is not uncommon to see people support themselves with their hands and twist their torsos when sitting down.

TIPTOES

When going on tiptoes correctly, the weight that is placed on the middle of the feet when standing (see section on "Standing") is placed on the balls of the feet, as the head leads the body to go forwards and upwards. It is important to maintain the alignment between the head, the neck and the back. The breath is not held, and the eyes are alert.

If you need to reach up towards something, remember to allow the hand to lead the arm, taking care not to push the shoulder up and out of the back (see section on "Reaching and Handling" for guidance).

When you come down to standing after being on tiptoes, think about releasing the heels gradually on to the ground, enabling your weight to be placed evenly on the middle of the feet. Take time to go over your primary directions.

▶ Look how this model is going on tiptoes to enable her hand to lead her arm to close the window.

◀ Here, the head, neck and back relationship is respected. The model is looking at the object without pulling her head back. The upper arms are widening as the hand leads the arm.

▶ Note how the head is pulled back, the lower back is pulled in, and the shoulder is raised to reach for the object, instead of allowing the hand to lead the arm.

◀ Note how the model is poised and aligned.

▶ See how the model's knees are braced and note the position of his legs as he pushes up to reach the lampshade to dust it. The head contraction is severe. The model is holding his breath, causing unnecessary tension throughout the body.

Reaching and Handling

Everyday activities frequently require the use of the arms and hands to reach out for or handle various objects. Whenever this is necessary, remember to maintain the alignment between the head, neck and back. If you are squatting to reach out for something, it is important for you to allow your hand to lead the movement.

▲ See how the model's weight is balanced over her feet, how she is widening across her upper arms, and how she is allowing her hand to lead her wrist and her arm.

▲ Here, the legs are straight and the head is pulled back, causing a lot of strain on the neck, and the shoulders are tensed. The arms are dragged forwards, causing the shoulder girdle to be rounded.

▲ Notice how this child is reaching out for her toy. Her head, her neck and her back are aligned. As she looks down towards the rattle, she hinges forwards from her hip joints.

▲ Here the model is reaching into the wardrobe (closet). She is allowing her arms to be supported by her back and maintaining her alignment.

▲ Here the model is pulling her head back and twisting her torso. She is standing on the right hip, thus compromising her balance.

▲ Look at how the model is standing. Her arms remain well connected to her shoulder blades and her back. She is holding the lamp without any undue tension in her arms and her wrists.

"MONKEY" OR BENDING

The position known as "monkey" enables us to move with more flexibility in our daily activities. It is a useful means of moving from standing to sitting or squatting, as well as helping with lifting, picking things up, working at a desk, washing, ironing, and participating in sports such as skiing and golf. The "monkey" position respects the relationship between the head, the neck and the back.

In "monkey" the head goes forwards and up and the knees go forwards and away over the feet to counterbalance the bottom going back over the heels, and enabling the arms to move freely.

When you go into "monkey" remember to review your primary directions. It is important to be alert and not to fix your gaze or hold your breath.

Stand with the legs hip-width apart, with the feet slightly turned outwards. Your weight should be evenly distributed, neither too far forwards nor too far back on your feet. To start going into "monkey", allow the knees to bend slightly over your feet as you tilt forwards from your hip joints, making sure your head, your neck and your back are aligned. Avoid collapsing over yourself!

▲ When going into "monkey" avoid retracting the head back and down into the spine. Note how the model has rounded her shoulders and pulled in her knees.

▲ Here the model is not bending her knees as she bends forwards. Her back is collapsed over her body, and her legs are straight and braced.

One final point is to make sure you think of widening and lengthening your back as you widen across the shoulder girdle, to allow free movement and your arms to hang freely.

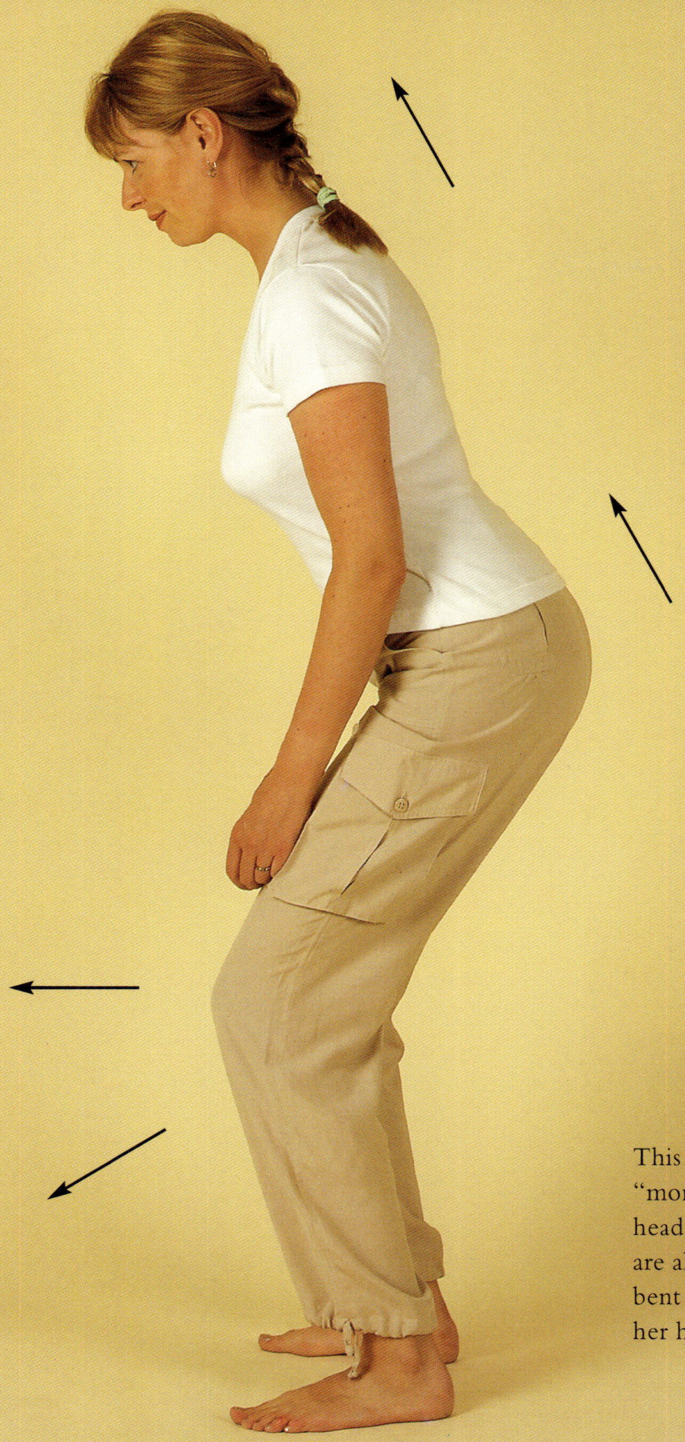

This model is in the correct "monkey" position. Her head, her neck and her back are aligned. Her knees are bent forward and away from her hips.

"MONKEY" OR BENDING – EVERYDAY SITUATIONS

In everyday situations it is important to pause before reacting, to enable yourself to be positioned in such a way as not to misuse yourself. The more conscious you are, the more likely you are to encourage muscular release throughout the whole of the system.

Equally, the more at peace you are within yourself, the easier you will find it to apply the principles of the technique. The following pictures illustrate some of the ways where "monkey" can be useful to maintain good use.

▲ Note how the model's back is aligned, how she is using her joints and allowing her widening arms to handle the dish.

▲ Here the model is pulling her head back. Her back is rounded, her legs braced and her arms are tense.

◀ See how the model is using the whole of his back correctly, allowing his weight to come back on to his heels and his knees to go forwards and away over his feet.

▶ Here, he is pulling his head back, rounding the back and holding in the arms.

▲ In this incorrect procedure, the man is collapsing from his waist down to make a curved border in the garden. His shoulders are rounded, his head pulled back.

▲ In this correct procedure, the model is poised and aligned to do her ironing. Her hand, wrist and arm are free as she holds the iron. She is also widening across her upper arms.

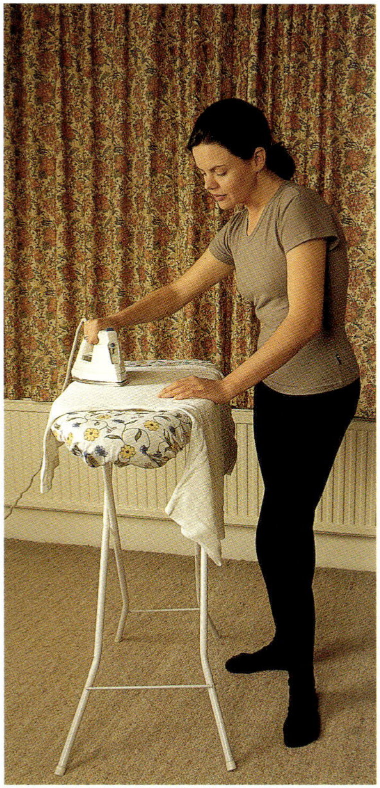

▲ Here, illustrating the incorrect procedure, the model is twisted to the right. Her hand and arm are tense.

"Lunge Monkey"

The procedure "lunge monkey" is similar to "monkey" in that the knees go forwards and away and the torso tilts slightly forwards from the hip joints. One foot is placed behind the other. The legs are placed precisely hip-width apart, enabling you to balance the upper part of your body on to the forward leg or the back leg whenever the need arises. In this way, your weight is displaced forwards or backwards according to your activity.

The "lunge monkey" is extremely useful when you need to lift something heavy from the floor, when you need to move objects from one side of a surface to another such as during cooking, or when you need to push or pull something.

When you go into "lunge monkey" it is important to remember to keep your head, your neck and your back aligned. The legs are hip-width apart. The arms hang freely on either side of the torso.

Allow your weight to move to the right on to the right foot (or to the left, as the situation demands. If moving to the left, reverse "right" and "left" in the following instructions).

Place your left foot forwards, slightly turned out at an angle. Then allow the left knee to bend forward, thus bringing the weight over on to the front foot. The right knee is slightly bent, as is the upper part of the body. Think about widening across the upper arms and the shoulder girdle, making sure the arms are not stiffening and are free to move if necessary. To come back on to the back leg, slowly bring the weight back from the left leg and place it on the right leg, making sure that you come back in one clean, smooth movement along the same plane.

You can transfer your weight from the front leg to the back leg either by coming back and up, or by coming back and down and back up again, depending on the level you need to reach. This maintains harmony between the bones and the muscles and allows your body to move freely.

▲ See how the model has collapsed from the waist down. Her shoulders are rounded. The legs are straight and the knees are braced, causing tension.

Observe how the model has gone into "lunge monkey". Her head, her neck and her back are aligned. Her knees are going forward and away from her hips.

"Lunge Monkey" – Everyday Situations

As with "monkey", the "lunge monkey" can give you more flexibility and a wider range of movement in everyday activities. It will enable you to adapt your environment to your needs, rather than the reverse, by placing yourself at the same level as the surfaces you need to work from.

"Lunge monkey" offers a wide range of possibilities, from vacuum cleaning to washing the car, and it is useful for chores such as making a bed.

▲ Note how this model is holding the vacuum cleaner. He is aligned, tilting slightly forwards from the hip joints. His knees are bent. One leg is placed behind the other, giving him flexibility to move forwards and backwards while he holds the vacuum handle.

▲ See how the model above is collapsing over the vacuum cleaner. He has lost the alignment between his head, his neck and his back, and is using unnecessary force to hold the vacuum handle.

◀ Note how the model is using himself in such a way as to maintain his alignment while washing his car. He is tilted forwards, giving himself a greater range of movement. His arms are free, supported by his back.

▶ See how the model this time is bending forwards from the waist. His legs are braced. His head is pulled back.

▲ As this model looks into the engine of his car, he is supported by his back. His legs are bent, giving him more flexibility to adjust himself.

▲ Note how the model here is restricting himself. Collapsed from his waist, his legs are braced. He is therefore limiting his range of movement.

▲ Note how this model has aligned herself to make the bed. Her legs are bent, enabling a greater range of movement.

▲ This time the model is collapsing from the waist down. Her legs are braced, her head is retracting back and down on to her spine.

Squatting or Lunge Squatting

In Western societies most people find it difficult to squat in their everyday lives. Young children have very little difficulty in doing so, but as we grow older we lose the flexibility to squat as our joints become less mobile.

A low "monkey" or semi-squat is the best way that an Alexander teacher can re-introduce a student to squatting over a series of lessons.

To squat, follow the same guidelines as for "monkey", but with a wider stance. Remember to maintain the alignment between the head, the neck and the back and to allow the joints in the hips, the knees and the ankles to be free. As you go into a deeper squat you might find that your heels come off the ground. This does not present a problem as far as the technique is concerned so long as you can keep your balance. As a general rule, go only as far as you feel comfortable.

Squatting is an extremely useful technique to adopt when you need to pick something off the floor, take something from a low drawer or lift up a child. An alternative can be lunge squatting. Follow the guidelines for "lunge monkey", bearing in mind that you need a wider stance.

To come up from deep squatting or lunge squatting into standing it is important to remember to lead with the head and to avoid pushing up with the legs as the back goes over the heels.

▲ Note how the model has lost the alignment with her back as she squats. Her head is dropped, and her shoulders are rounded.

▲ Here the model is lunge squatting incorrectly. The head retraction is severe, her shoulders are raised and her arms braced even though she has one of her legs placed behind the other.

In this correct procedure, observe how the model's head, neck and back are aligned. Her shoulders are widening across her upper arms.

Squatting or Lunge Squatting – Everyday Situations

It is very easy to continue using inappropriate positioning to deal with the demands of everyday life situations. Picking things up from low surfaces is no exception. End-gaining attitudes die hard!

Once again, pause and think before doing anything, to avoid reverting to familiar patterns, such as bending from the waist and bracing in the legs. The following photographs illustrate some of the pitfalls that you can learn to avoid and guidelines on how to improve your use in given situations.

▲ Here the model is squatting correctly. Her head, her neck and her back are aligned. She is widening across her upper arms, allowing them to be integrated into her back.

▲ In this incorrect example, note how the model is retracting his head and collapsing from the waist down.

◀ This model is lunge squatting to brush something up from the floor. She has maintained her good use, giving herself a maximum range of movement.

▶ Here, in an incorrect example of how you should sweep the floor, the model is restricting his range of movement.

▲ Note how the woman above is squatting by maintaining the alignment between her head, her neck and her back, making eye contact to call the puppy towards her.

▲ This time the woman is collapsing from the waist down. Her legs are braced, and her head is pulled back.

◀ Note how this man is squatting to plant a rose bush in his garden. By placing himself at the same level as the rose, he is allowing himself a greater range of movement.

On All Fours

All fours and crawling are helpful procedures, as they encourage the back to lengthen and widen, as well as encouraging the co-ordination of the head, the neck, the back and the limbs.

▼ When on all fours, remember to maintain the alignment between the head, the neck and the back. Your weight should be evenly distributed between your legs and your arms. Avoid bracing your arms.

▲ Note how the model is over-arching her back and dropping her head. Her toes are tucked in, causing unnecessary tension in her toes.

▲ In this example the model is pulling her head back and causing unnecessary strain on her neck.

To go down on all fours, kneel, then walk your hands forwards in front of you in such a way that the head leads and the torso follows. The hands should be placed palms down on the floor, and the arms should be shoulder-width apart. Your legs and knees should be positioned under your hip joints. You should be giving yourself your primary directions.

To get up from all fours, move your bottom towards your heels as you walk your hands back. You can go into standing from a kneeling position or alternatively go into a squat and follow the procedures previously described.

CRAWLING

To crawl, the same principles apply as for being on all fours. Remember to lead with the head as you do cross-pattern (opposite arms and legs) crawling.

▶ Watch how a baby crawls efficiently and quickly around a room.

▲ When crawling, avoid narrowing your stance by bringing the knees too close together, as this tends to narrow the back.

▲ Note how the model is dropping her head and rounding her shoulders as she is crawling, and how her knees are too close together.

Walking

Walking, like any other activity, should be consciously directed. As the head leads and the body is aligned, the legs follow. It is important that our eyes remain alert to our surroundings, as too much focus within cuts us off from our environment. Be careful not to wear clothes that restrict your movements. Tight trousers, jeans or skirts impair our breathing. Likewise, high-heeled shoes tend to make us pull the lower back in, and usually shorten the muscles in the back of the legs. Do not constrict the feet and especially the toes by wearing tight shoes.

▲ Here the model hunches her shoulders and holds in her arms. She has dropped her head to look down, instead of looking ahead.

▲ In this correct example, the head leads the movement, and the arms are free to move, enabling the legs to follow.

▲ Here the model has lost the alignment between her head, her neck and her back by allowing the head to drop at the neckline.

Walking Upstairs or Downstairs

◀ Think about your primary directions, to allow the whole of the body to lengthen. Leading with the head propels the body upwards and uses a minimum of energy.

▶ Here the model is slumping and looking down, requiring far more effort to move her body and legs.

◀ By allowing the head to be poised and the whole of the torso to lengthen along the front, the model moves in a free and more balanced way.

▶ The model looks down and slumps forwards, and has to hold in her legs to avoid losing her balance. More energy is needed to support the system.

Lifting

A lot of back pain is the result of frequent lifting of heavy weights. To avoid unnecessary strain on the back, stand as near to the load as possible by placing your feet on either side of it. Remember to maintain the alignment between your head, your neck and your back. Go into "monkey" or "lunge monkey" as far down as necessary in order to move into a squat or lunge squat (see previous sections on "Squatting or Lunge Squatting" for details). Bend your arms so that your elbows are close to your body.

Make sure that you widen across the upper arms as you place your hands on the load, and hold firmly without gripping the hands or tensing in the arms or wrists. If the arms, wrists and hands are tense you will lose the contact with your lower back.

▼Once you are holding the load as closely to your body as you can, come out of a squat or lunge squat into a "monkey" or a "lunge monkey", before standing.

▲ To place the load back on the ground, reverse the process and apply the same principles, making sure that your head, your neck and your back are aligned, your arms are free, and your hips and knees are bent.

▲ This model incorrectly drops her head, braces her legs and rounds her back to put down a load.

▲ This model incorrectly braces her arms, rounds her back and pulls her head back while lifting.

CARRYING

When carrying shopping bags, or luggage, avoid holding everything in one hand. Such action will cause you to start pulling down on one side of the body or the other. Think about evenly distributing the weight between both arms. Avoid bracing the arms and narrowing across the upper arms. Avoid bracing the arms and hunching. (See sections on "Walking" and "Standing" for guidance.)

▲ This model is carrying her shopping bags so that they are evenly distributed on both sides.

▲ Here the model is carrying all of her shopping bags in one hand, creating an imbalance as she pulls down to the left. She is raising her right shoulder in an attempt to support her handbag.

▼ This model is aligned while carrying his briefcase.

◀ Here, the model is pulling down to the right. His shoulders are no longer parallel. He is holding his briefcase with unnecessary tension in the arms.

▲ Look at the way this mother is carrying her child. Her weight is evenly distributed and she is holding the child close to her body, supporting his upper and lower body firmly.

▲ Note how this mother is carrying her child on her hip. She has lost her alignment. Her weight is displaced unevenly on her hip, creating strain.

READING AND WRITING

When reading it is important to spend some time considering how you will sit to avoid slumping, which is very easy to do, especially in armchairs or on sofas. Likewise, it is very easy to get drawn into what you read and to forget about your posture altogether. Long periods of immobility can create unnecessary tension and discomfort in your body so it is important to be sitting correctly to begin with.

▲ A useful solution when reading is to use a sloping board to avoid slumping over your desk or table. It is interesting to note that in the days when clerks were employed to write up ledgers by hand, they used sloping desks. Take short breaks to avoid stiffening throughout your body.

▲ Note how the model has lost her alignment and contact with her sitting bones. Look at how she is holding her body with her arm, and how her legs are folded, offering her no support.

When you are sitting at your desk or at a table (see section on "Sitting" for guidelines), it is important to adjust your chair in such a way that your lower arms and hands can be placed on the surface of your table or desk at a right angle. If your chair is too close you are likely to lift your shoulders to adjust your arms. If your chair is too high, you will probably start slumping. Avoid crossing your legs and make sure your feet are flat on the floor.

▶ Your pad or paper should be placed in front of you so that you do not need to overreach to use them. With your head leading, tilt forward from your hip joints, bearing in mind that you need to maintain the alignment between your head, your neck and your back.

▲ Note how this model is firmly gripping the pen, causing tension in her wrist and hand.

▲ Here the model is tensing in her wrist, her hand and her arm, restricting her movement.

DESKWORK

An increasing number of people are complaining of neck and shoulder tension, wrist problems and back pain resulting from their working environment. Many reasons can be found for this. Some cases are linked to poorly designed furniture, awkward or unfavourable sitting positions and immobility. In other instances, although chairs and work surfaces are good, posture is poor.

▲ Here, the spine is aligned, and the head poised on top. The feet are on the floor.

▲ See how the model is sitting. Slumping causes unnecessary tension in the spine and weakens the muscles surrounding the torso.

It is important to remember your primary directions. The head, the neck and the back should be aligned. The head is lengthening away from the sitting bones.

Your office or work chair should be tilted slightly forward and adjusted so that your feet are flat on the floor. Your upper arms should be widening away from each other and your forearms should be positioned horizontally. Remember that comfortable and supportive office chairs can never compensate for poor posture.

It is also important to avoid overreaching when you need to get something on a different part of your desk or in a drawer.

▲ A useful aid if you are writing for long periods is to use a wedge-shaped cushion to give you plenty of support in the pelvis and spine.

▲ Here the model is overreaching to write on his pad. He is supporting himself with his elbow, and his feet are no longer fully in contact with the floor.

USE OF THE TELEPHONE

When using the telephone it is very easy to forget about good use and to start moving down towards the receiver while you are talking. The stimulus to answer the telephone quickly, in what is often a stressful environment at the office or at home, is very strong indeed. Remember to take time to stop and consider your directions before answering.

Compare how the models in the pictures are holding their telephones:

OBSERVE YOURSELF WHEN THE TELEPHONE RINGS

Do you grab it? Or do you try to give yourself some time before you pick it up?
Next time the telephone rings, stop and go over your primary directions.
Make sure you bring the receiver to your ear rather than leaning down towards it, thus compromising your use.

▲ In this case the model is aligned. Her shoulders are widening away from each other.

▲ Here the model is holding the mobile phone against her ear, supported by her shoulder.

◀ In this case the model has maintained her balance throughout her body.

▶ Here the model is pulling her head down towards her mobile phone to talk.

◀ In this case the model is holding the telephone with his left hand and preserving his alignment.

▶ Here the telephone is placed on the left-hand side and is being held with the right hand, causing a twist to the right.

WORKING AT A COMPUTER

When you are working at a computer terminal or portable computer, it is important to remember to sit adequately at your desk (see section on "Sitting" for guidance). Your feet should be placed on the ground, your knees directed over your feet and your weight evenly distributed on both sitting bones to avoid straining the lower back. You should be aware of the alignment between your head, your neck and your back. As you place your hands on the keyboard, you might need to tip slightly forwards.

▲ Chairs that tilt forwards slightly can help you maintain good posture. You can also buy a wedge-shaped cushion to give you extra support in the pelvis and spine area.

▲ If you are working at a computer or portable computer, use your eyes to look down towards it. Avoid breaking at the neck as you will lose the alignment with your back.

It is important not to overreach with the arms. Check that your forearms are in a horizontal position, and align the lower arms and the wrists so as not to compromise the width across the upper arms. The keyboard should be just below elbow height. Avoid holding in your shoulders or arms, as this will probably cause unnecessary muscular tension, and you risk losing the contact with your lower back. As with all activity, it is very easy to stop being aware of good use, so remember to take short breaks to relieve your muscles and improve your circulation. Bring your attention back to yourself regularly to check that you are not slumping or being drawn into your computer!

▲ Here the model collapses over her computer. She has lost the alignment between her hands, her wrists and her lower arms. Her shoulders are hunched.

▲ Here the model is holding in her wrist, arms and shoulders, causing unnecessary strain and discomfort.

DRIVING

Most of the problems experienced by drivers are due to fixed postures, long journeys and poor sitting support.

Many people who spend a considerable amount of time driving will usually find themselves constricted by the position of the steering wheel and the pedals. Such a cramped environment is bound to lead to stress and strain on the back and equally on the arms and legs.

When choosing a car take time to see whether the seat is firm and supportive. If you already own a car and it does not have a lumbar support adjustment, you can use a wedge-shaped cushion to give you adequate support in the lumbar area and the pelvis. This in turn will improve the alignment of your spine, your neck and your head. Make sure that the back of the seat is in an upright position and that you do not lock your arms, wrists and hands.

▲ You should be able to reach the pedals easily. A wedge-shaped cushion is useful to avoid slumping.

▲ See how the model is collapsing, how the head is pulled forward and the arms are fixed.

When driving long distances, make sure you take regular breaks. Give yourself plenty of time to arrive at your destination so as to avoid anxiety and unnecessary stress on the system.

Be careful not to twist your torso when you get into the car. As you get out, turn the whole of your body towards the car door, then swing your legs out so that your feet are on the ground. Lead with your head as you stand up.

As you get in, sit on the edge of the car seat and then turn the whole of your torso into the car as you swing your legs inside the vehicle.

Unloading and Loading the Car

When loading and unloading your car, be careful to place the heaviest items or loads nearest to you in the boot (trunk). This will prevent overreaching into the boot, which can lead to holding and stiffening in the arms and a loss of the connection into the back and legs.

Make sure you go with a "lunge monkey", and that you carry your load as close to your body as possible (see sections on "Lunge Monkey", "Lifting" and "Carrying" for guidance). In this way you will avoid straining unnecessarily and tensing your muscles.

▲ See how this man is maintaining the alignment between his head, neck and back. He has gone into a "lunge monkey" to give himself more flexibility in his range of movements.

▲ Here he is collapsing forwards. His shoulders are rounded, and his legs straight and braced.

DRINKING AND EATING

If you are standing while you are drinking remember to be alert, not to fix your gaze, and ensure that your head leads you away from your heels (see section on "Standing" for guidance). The shoulder girdle brings mobility to the arms, and the pelvis provides stability, which allows mobility in the legs.

▲ Avoid gripping or clutching your glass. Be aware of the connection with your arm, which links into your back, then into your heels. As you raise the cup to your lips, bring your weight back onto the heels, so as not to pull in your lower back. Think about lengthening the front of your torso, so as not to compromise your length. Bring the glass to the lips, rather than leaning down into it with the head.

▲ See how the model is unbalanced while she is drinking, and how she is pulling in her lower back.

▲ Note how the model's head is leaning down towards her drink, and how her shoulders are rounded.

The same principles for drinking correctly, as described opposite, also apply to eating. Whether you are going to eat something from your hand or use a fork, it is very easy to forget your posture altogether, to start end-gaining and to become solely focused on your food!

▲ Take some time to consider how you are seated at your table and bring your food to your mouth, rather than the reverse. The feet should be positioned on the floor. You should be aware of both your sitting bones and your back should be lengthening and widening.

▲ Note how this model is sitting at the table while eating. She is slumped, and her head is leaning downwards in order to reach the food. This will create unnecessary pressure on the spine as the head retraction is severe.

Index

Michèle Mac Donnell (MSTAT) gives Alexander Technique lessons in London and can be contacted on: 0171 792 5287.